LOLA
BERRY'S
little book of
SMOOTHIES
& JUICES

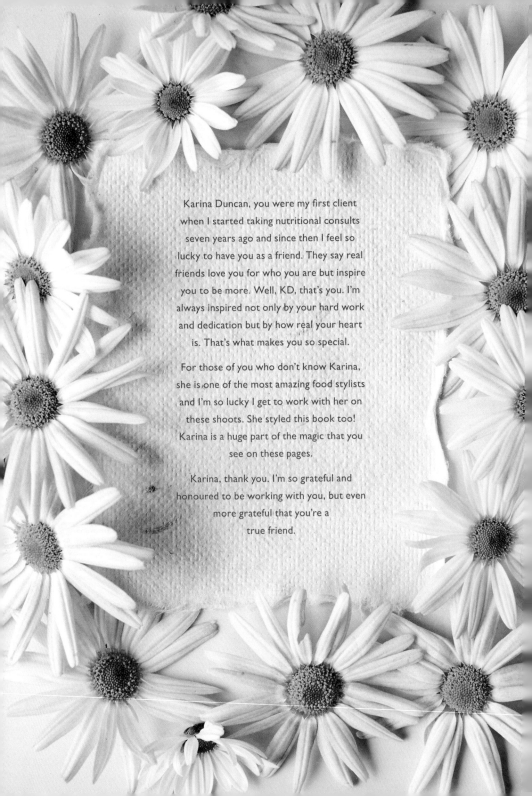

Karina Duncan, you were my first client
when I started taking nutritional consults
seven years ago and since then I feel so
lucky to have you as a friend. They say real
friends love you for who you are but inspire
you to be more. Well, KD, that's you. I'm
always inspired not only by your hard work
and dedication but by how real your heart
is. That's what makes you so special.

For those of you who don't know Karina,
she is one of the most amazing food stylists
and I'm so lucky I get to work with her on
these shoots. She styled this book too!
Karina is a huge part of the magic that you
see on these pages.

Karina, thank you. I'm so grateful and
honoured to be working with you, but even
more grateful that you're a
true friend.

LOLA BERRY'S
little book of
SMOOTHIES
& JUICES

plum.

Pan Macmillan Australia

Contents

Introduction

First up, this little creation is for you, to help make putting your health first just that little bit easier. With our fast-paced, stressful lives, looking after our health often gets put on the back burner. I get it, trust me: I, too, fall off the wagon when I'm stressed out or time-poor. Unfortunately, eating on autopilot often seems easier than planning a healthy meal.

But you know what? When you make your health a priority you can handle stress and all the ups and downs of life so much better. Being healthy means you're more on your A-game and can make better use of each and every experience. So here's to making the choice to put your health first, thriving, glowing and feeling alive.

This little book contains 60 smoothie and juice recipes, broken down by colour, that you can make up in a jiffy. You can even make them in advance! Often I'll whip up a big batch of a delicious, nourishing smoothie and it will last me for three brekkies in a row. In fact, all of these recipes will last three days in the fridge, so no more excuses! Being too time-poor to be healthy can now be a thing of the past.

I hope this smoothie and juice collection inspires you to try something new, empowers you to be the best version of yourself and, most importantly, makes you happy. These are all recipes that make me smile, and I'm rapt I get to share them with you. Oh, and they're all dairy- and gluten-free, and there are plenty of vegan options too.

So pull that blender or juicer out of the cupboard and get experimenting. These recipes are just guides to get you going – if you want to remove an ingredient, or swap hazelnuts for macadamia nuts, well, that's totally fine. This is your life, your tastebuds, your body, and your health … so make it work for you.

At the end of the day, choosing to be healthy isn't about going on some super-strict detox. Believe me, I've been there, and it's not much fun and is often very short-lived. It's all about choosing to be healthy because you want to do it, for no one else but you. I believe in you, but at the end of the day, that doesn't matter. It doesn't matter if you have a whole gang of souls believing in you; the trick is to believe in yourself. You've totally got this.

What You'll Need

Blenders

Sometimes I put nuts and dried seaweed into my smoothie combos, which can be a little tricky for a hand mixer (like a Bamix) or a standard blender, so I use a Vitamix. This makes my smoothies super silky, so that even though their colour may be monstersnot green, they'll taste great, and their texture will be perfect. Get the best blender you can afford, because the end result in terms of texture, flavour and consistency will be so worth it!

When you're making smoothies, depending on the ingredients, your processing time can be anywhere from 1 to 3 minutes. Sometimes I will blend everything up, and then give it another 30 seconds at the end to make sure it's nice and creamy. Generally, the longer you blend it, the smoother the consistency.

Juicers

There's a wide range of juicers on the market from basic machines to the expensive heavy-duty pulverizers seen in juice bars. Most juicers are 'centrifugal extractors', where fruit and veggies are pushed down a tube into a spinning basket with a powerful grater at the base. The pulp is shredded and trapped, while the juice pours out of the side. Then you've got the slower 'masticating' juicers that chew the food up and extract the juice with the pulp popping out like a little sausage. As a general rule, the more expensive the juicer is the bigger its motor will be, so the better it'll be at extracting the juice – particularly from tougher ingredients like beetroot, pumpkin or kale.

To maximise the flavour and health benefits, keep the skin on all of your fruit and veggies (except bananas, oranges, grapefruit, pineapple and melons) when juicing. Yes, that means leaving the skin on your kiwifruit, lemons and limes – it may be a little bitter but that's where so much of the goodness is! Just make sure you give all your fruit and veggies a really good rinse first and trim any ends, as well as chopping them into smaller pieces to help feed them through the machine if you need to. Juices are a ripper way to get more nutrients into your diet, and once you're in the habit of making one every couple of days you'll find that you crave them.

Milk Alternatives

I often use coconut water and almond milk in my smoothies, but there are heaps of milk alternatives, such as milk made from oats, rice, cashews, macadamia nuts, quinoa and hazelnuts. It's easy to make your own if you have a really good food processor. The ratio is 1 cup of nuts to 2 cups of water. (You'll need to soak them overnight first, and give them a good rinse.) Strain through a fine mesh sieve and you're done! (You can save the fibrous bits and use them for a raw treat recipe, or simply add them to a granola mix.) If you don't have time to make your own nut milk, you can buy it off the shelf. Just read the labels and stay away from the stuff with loads of sugars or sweeteners. And watch out for preservatives. There should be about four ingredients and you should be able to pronounce all of them. If you can't (or they are just numbers), look them up to see if they come from a natural source.

Sweetener Options

Sweeteners are another ingredient in my smoothies that you can easily change to suit you. There's coconut nectar, maple syrup, stevia, dates, figs, agave, raw honey, rice syrup, coconut palm sugar, rapadura (also called penala) monk fruit extract and yacon syrup — have I forgotten anything? Remember that even natural sweeteners should only be used to slightly sweeten something; they shouldn't be guzzled down just because you bought them from a health food store. I fell into that trap before I understood my body. I used to eat whole packets of dates and used stacks of agave in my smoothies. Never again.

If you can't tolerate too much fructose then you need to be careful with sweeteners such as agave and honey. My advice? Try a little first. Some people don't like the aftertaste of stevia, although I quite enjoy it. It's about trying things out and finding what works best for you. If you feel bloated, grumpy or lethargic after using a particular sweetener, try something else.

Smoothie Toppers

These smoothie topper combos are an easy way to make your smoothies more interesting. Mix up a few of these on a weekend and keep in jars ready to top your smoothies during the week. These little recipes should give you about 6 serves.

- ½ cup each of sunflower seeds, pumpkin seeds and dried cranberries
- ½ cup each of goji berries and roughly chopped walnuts
- ½ cup each of chia seeds, roughly chopped almonds and dried blueberries
- ½ cup each of shredded coconut, pumpkin seeds and white mulberries or goji berries
- ½ cup each of roughly chopped Brazil nuts, pecans and bee pollen
- ½ cup each of pistachios and dried cranberries, ¼ cup shredded coconut
- ½ cup each of sunflower seeds, shredded coconut and dried pomegranate seeds or goji berries
- ½ cup each of roughly chopped walnuts and dried figs, ¼ cup rolled oats, a pinch of nutmeg and ¼ teaspoon ground cinnamon
- ½ cup cacao nibs, ¼ cup chia seeds
- ½ cup goji berries, ¼ cup shredded coconut

These are also easy-peasy toppers, but need to be made fresh so are good for one or two smoothies at a time.

- ¼ cup roughly chopped macadamia nuts mixed with zest of ½ a lemon
- 1 teaspoon chopped mint leaves and 2 tablespoons goji berries

Notes on the Recipes

Wherever possible, all the foods I eat and use in my recipes are whole, raw, organic, seasonal, unprocessed and as close to their natural state as possible. This means that, where I can, I keep the skins on my fruit and veg and try to use the whole thing (though I make sure to give them a good rinse and a trim and remove any pips or stones first!), chopping up the ingredients only where I need to in order to get them into the blender or juicer. If you can, I suggest you do the same. You'll also notice that I use frozen bananas in lots of my smoothies. That's because I love the texture and sweetness they give, plus, they've got a bit more glucose than fructose, so people with fructose malabsorption can often tolerate small serves. Just don't forget to peel your narnies before you freeze them — it's no fun trying to do this afterwards!

All the smoothies and juices in this book will make enough for 2 and will keep in the fridge for up to 3 days.

Essential Ingredients

Acai Berry Powder

Made from the purple berries of the acai tree native to the Amazon rainforest, this powder is jam-packed with antioxidants, vitamins, calcium, iron and amino acids. It's not very sweet straight up, so it makes a great addition to a smoothie or an 'acai bowl' together with lots of other fruits, seeds and granola.

Almond Butter

This ground almond paste, with all its lovely oils, is a wonderful butter substitute. I prefer mine raw (not roasted) because it's the healthier option. Almonds are loaded with fibre, good fats and protein, plus they've got a fair bit of magnesium and calcium.

Almond Milk

You can add unsweetened almond milk to pretty much any recipe that calls for milk. You can make your own almond milk if you have a powerful food processor.

Avocados

Avocados are a good source of fibre, potassium and vitamin C, and although they are high in fat, it's the good kind (unsaturated, like olive oil). My favourite variety is Hass, which is available all year round.

Bee Pollen

Bee pollen is the soft yellow 'dust' from flowers that bees brush into the pollen sacs on their back legs. Bees use it to feed their larvae and to make royal jelly and it's high in protein and nutrients. It makes a great smoothie topper, though try not to go too nuts on it as it takes a bee working 8 hours a day an entire month to produce just one teaspoon of pollen. People with pollen allergies should avoid bee pollen and vegans might prefer to leave it out too.

Cacao

Technically, cacao and cocoa are the same thing, but in everyday use, cacao usually refers to the raw, unprocessed beans, and cocoa to the beans that are roasted and processed (and usually combined with milk and sugar to make chocolate). Raw cacao powder is the healthiest way to give your smoothies a chocolate hit. It's delicious and full of health benefits, especially for our brains. It's high in magnesium (great for our muscles and heart) and phenylalanine, a precursor to two brain chemicals that make us feel good (norepinephrine and dopamine) – maybe that's why we love chocolate so much! Cacao nibs are crushed unroasted cacao beans and are great for adding to smoothies at the last minute for a texture and flavour boost.

Carob Powder

Carob powder is delicious, with a sweet, chocolate-like taste. It's a great source of fibre and minerals including calcium and magnesium. It's also great for digestion and was traditionally used for settling upset stomachs. Sometimes I switch it for cacao in my smoothies when I want my chocolate flavour nice and subtle and when I don't want to be shaken up by the stimulants (caffeine and theobromine) that are found in regular cacao. Carob is an acquired taste but personally, I love the stuff!

Chia Seeds

Chia seeds provide an amazing hit of nutrients, especially protein, calcium and omega-3 fatty acids. I like to sprinkle them on top of my smoothies. To get the full benefits, soak the seeds – even five minutes is enough.

Chilli

Chillies speed up your metabolic rate (good for weight control), promote heart health, and are full of antioxidants (great for your skin). The mildest chilli is the longish, thin cayenne chilli (it comes in red, green and yellow), followed by the medium–hot ball chilli, the hot jalapeño, the very hot tiny bird's eye chilli and the scorching habañero. I like to add a tiny pinch of chilli flakes to my smoothies and have used the milder cayenne chillies for the recipes in this book.

Coconut Milk and Coconut Cream

These are great for smoothies. Coconut milk and cream are made the same way, just using different amounts of water. You can make them yourself or buy them ready-made. If possible, buy organic coconut cream packed in BPA-free tins (BPA is a toxic chemical that works like oestrogen and can affect your hormones). There are also a few 'drinking coconut milks' out there, which are lighter and have a higher water content. I love using these when I want my smoothies to be a tad lighter. It's totally your call – try them out and see what works for you.

Coconut Oil

People worry about coconut oil making them fat. It is a saturated fat and is solid at cooler temperatures, but it's also a medium-chain fatty acid, which means the body can use it quickly (rather than having to store it). It's also thermogenic, meaning it helps to speed up your metabolism. I tell my clients to pop a teaspoonful into their morning smoothies or teas. It's awesome used topically, too – I use it to moisturise my face and body.

Coconut Nectar

This has a slightly stronger flavour than honey or even agave – almost like a mild molasses. It's loaded with minerals and contains less fructose than agave and honey, too. But remember, it's still a sweetener, so use it in moderation.

Coconut Water

Coconut water is the liquid from young coconuts and it's a bit like Mother Nature's very own electrolyte drink. It's naturally sweet and makes a fantastic base for smoothies . If you're a cocktail fan, then it's also great mixed with your favourite alcohol (and the electrolytes will help to prevent a hangover!).

Dried Coconut

You can get desiccated, that's super-fine; then there's shredded, which is long, thin pieces; and flaked, which is chunky and chewy.

Goji Berries

These berries are a great source of antioxidants and have a nice flavour – not too sweet, a bit like a sour-ish sultana. They are great added to smoothies before blending or sprinkled over the top to finish.

Herbs and Spices

Fresh herbs and spices can work wonders in adding flavour to your smoothies, not to mention the antioxidant hit you'll reap from them. Some of my favourites are: cinnamon, coriander, mint, nutmeg, chilli flakes, cardamom and turmeric. The list goes on!

Honey, Raw

Raw honey has been filtered, but in a way that doesn't destroy its nutrients. It is not pasteurized (the heating and filtration process that makes it clear), so all its beneficial enzymes are still present. Raw honey can be solid at room temperature (depending on how cold it is), and is usually milky (not clear). It's about twice as sweet as sugar, so you don't need to use as much.

Lavender, Dried

Lavender is a sweet herb native to Northern Africa and the mountains of the Mediterranean. When you think of lavender you might think of beauty products and soaps but it's actually so much more than that – with its anti-inflammatory and antiseptic qualities it's also used to treat wounds topically and the bit I love is that it helps to calm the nervous system, easing insomnia, depression and anxiety. I like to pop a few sprigs on my pillow for a good night's sleep.

Linseed (Flaxseed)

Linseed (also called flaxseed) is a great source of fibre, and is high in omega-3 fatty acids and minerals. I always tell my vegan clients to up the flaxseeds and flaxseed oil. You can get brown flax and golden flax, but both contain the same nutrients. To really release the nutrients, the seeds need to be ground up. I never bake or cook with linseed as heat destroys its nutrients.

LSA

LSA stands for (ground) linseed, sunflower and almond, and is an awesome superfood perfect for use in my smoothies. It's high in fibre, good fats and veggo protein, plus it has a nice hit of B vitamins.

Macadamia Nuts and Oil

Macadamia nuts are an excellent source of monounsaturated fats and a top brain food. I love the texture and flavour they add to smoothies. Macadamia oil is so pure I even use it on my skin.

Maca Powder

Also known as Peruvian ginseng, maca powder has been used in Peru for endurance, energy, hormonal balance and even as a libido enhancer for thousands of years. I like to add it to my smoothies to give me a big old caffeine-free energy boost. I notice that my hair and nails get really strong when I have maca powder too.

Maple Syrup

Maple syrup is a wonderful sweetener with a great flavour. It's full of minerals and contains less fructose than honey, dates or agave. Just make sure you choose 100 per cent syrup, not the imitation stuff. It costs more, but it's much healthier.

Medjool Dates

Dates are a great source of the electrolyte potassium, which is a key player for heart health. Plus, they're full of fibre and will keep you regular. Medjool dates are bigger, sweeter and squidgier than regular dried dates.

Nut Milks

You can whip up your own nut milks easily; all you need is 1 cup of raw nuts (always use raw for nut milks), 2 cups water and a good blender – then whiz it up. Sometimes I add nutmeg and cinnamon so it's like a nut milk chai. And you can either keep the pulp in (it's full of fibre) or strain it with a nut milk bag or muslin cloth, then use that pulp to make a raw treat the next day.

Nuts and Seeds

Nuts and seeds are a brilliant source of good fats. When my recipes say to soak and rinse nuts, this means soak them in water for 2 hours or more (overnight if possible) then rinse. This removes enzyme inhibitors and makes them easier to digest. Even a 20-minute soak will have a positive effect.

Oats

Pure oats don't contain gluten, but because of the way we process them, most oatmeal brands have been cross-contaminated with miniscule amounts of wheat, barley and/ or rye, so we can't call them gluten free. About 30 per cent of people who have coeliac disease cannot tolerate oats (even when the cross-contamination is almost eliminated), so if you have coeliac disease, or a particularly severe gluten allergy, proceed with caution.

Olive Oil, Extra-virgin

Olive oil is a great source of monounsaturated fats. Just make sure the oil you buy is extra-virgin, which means it's been pressed once, with no chemicals or additives.

Pepitas (Pumpkin Seeds)

Pepitas are full of zinc, an important mineral for health. Zinc is found in every cell of our bodies and plays a big role in immunity, cell division, cell growth, wound healing and the breakdown of carbs.

Pomegranate

Pomegranate seeds are packed with anti-oxidants. Dried, they make great smoothie toppers. The juice is great, but make sure you get 100 per cent pure juice, otherwise it will have added sweeteners.

Rice Malt Syrup

A carbohydrate blend of glucose and maltose, rice malt syrup is a good sweetener alternative for those who have difficulty absorbing fructose. Made from cooked fermented rice, it is a relatively slow-release sweetener, which means it won't put as much of a load on the liver as pure glucose does and will be less likely to give you that sugar 'spike' that leads to soaring and crashing energy levels.

Salt

I love to use pink salt in my cooking and occasionally it finds a way into my smoothie recipes too. Pink salt tastes just like normal salt but has loads more minerals (about 84 trace minerals in fact). It's great to use in place of regular table salt and looks pretty. I use Murray River or Himalayan. Celtic salt and rock salt are healthy options, too. Always use salt sparingly though and stay away from the bleached stuff.

Spirulina Powder

Spirulina powder is extracted from algae and contains a super-rich source of proteins, vitamins, minerals, essential fatty acids and antioxidants. I like to add it to my smoothies for an extra energy and nutrient boost.

Stevia Extract

Stevia, which is made from the leaves of a South American herb, is about 300 times sweeter than sugar, has no calories and no impact on blood sugar levels. You can buy it in powder form or as a liquid. Use it sparingly – if you use more than a couple of drops of liquid you'll get a pretty nasty aftertaste. It doesn't taste quite the same as sugar, but once you're used to it, you'll be converted.

Tahini

Tahini is a paste made from crushed sesame seeds. You can buy hulled (where the seed casing has been removed) and unhulled (made from the whole seed). Both are high in protein and good fats. I tend to use hulled tahini in my smoothies as it has a milder taste, but unhulled has more calcium and fibre and works well too. You can also get black tahini, which tastes similar to hulled tahini.

Vanilla Pods

Vanilla bean pods, like honey and cinnamon, are a great libido enhancer. Wrap the pods in foil, seal them in a zip-lock bag, and store them in a cool, dark place so they don't dry out. Vanilla pods can be pricey, but you can always use powdered vanilla (make sure it's 100 per cent vanilla) or vanilla extract (not chemically produced essence) instead.

Dreamy

Greens

Super Green

I love, love, *love* green smoothies, and this is my new favourite. It's easy, so creamy and my go-to pick-me-up if I'm feeling burnt out.

large handful of chopped baby spinach or kale

80 g (½ cup) cashew nuts, soaked for 2 hours or overnight, then rinsed

1 avocado

1 frozen banana

1 vanilla pod, split and seeds scraped

2 tablespoons maple syrup

500 ml (2 cups) almond milk

pinch of ground cinnamon

cashew nuts, to serve

Throw the kale, cashews, avocado, banana, vanilla seeds, maple syrup, almond milk and cinnamon into the blender and whiz it all up until silky smooth (add a little extra almond milk if you feel it needs it – I like mine thick but it's about making it perfect for your taste buds).

Pour into glasses or bowls and top with a few extra cashew nuts. Delish!

Serves 2

TIPS
When freezing your bananas, remember to peel them first! Trust me: it's no fun trying to peel a frozen banana – you end up losing most of it because it's stuck to the skin. And don't sweat if you haven't had the time to soak the cashews, it won't affect the taste or texture, it just helps you digest all their nutrients.

Mighty Minty

>>>>-

This is one of the quickest and easiest ways to get some extra greens into your diet. It's a beauty for breakfast, lunch or even dinner. It will keep for about 3 days (though will discolour slightly without affecting the flavour) so make a big batch (double the ingredients) and top it each day with something different.

1 avocado

2 frozen bananas

large handful of baby spinach

handful of mint leaves

handful of coriander leaves and stalks

500 ml (2 cups) coconut water

Pop the lot in your blender and whiz until silky smooth (add more coconut water if it's too thick for you – I love to eat mine with a spoon).

Pour into bowls or glasses and top with your favourite goodies. I like granola, edible flowers, shredded coconut, crushed nuts, pepitas (pumpkin seeds), goji berries and bee pollen – the list goes on! – but you can use pretty much whatever tickles your fancy. A teaspoon of rolled oats is really nice, too.

Serves 2

Green Goods

We all know greens are stuffed full of health benefits and a smoothie like this is such a brilliant way to sneak loads of them into your diet. I love this super, *super* thick to the extent that I eat it from a bowl with a spoon, but you can always thin it down until you've got it just how you like it.

2 handfuls of baby spinach

1 frozen banana

handful of blueberries (fresh or frozen), plus extra to serve

½ avocado

1 tablespoon extra-virgin coconut oil, melted

250 ml (1 cup) almond milk

250 ml (1 cup) water (optional)

Pop the spinach, banana, blueberries, avocado, coconut oil and almond milk into the blender and whiz everything together until smooth, then add the water little by little to thin it out until it's just how you like it.

Pour into bowls (or glasses if you've thinned it a bit), sprinkle over some extra blueberries and enjoy!

Serves 2

Karma Kiwi Freeze

This is really icy cool and is great for a hot summer's night. It tastes almost like a dessert and is actually perfect for after dinner, as kiwifruit contain loads of enzymes that work wonders for your digestion.

handful of baby spinach

2 frozen kiwifruit

4 medjool dates, pitted

1 frozen banana

1 zucchini

500 ml (2 cups) coconut water

Pop everything into the blender and process until it looks like a Slurpee.

Pour it into bowls or glasses and enjoy.

Serves 2

TIPS
If you're not keen on kiwifruit skin, be sure to take it off before freezing as it can be hard to get off otherwise! I like to keep mine on to increase the health benefits, as lots of the nutrients can be found close to the skin. If you're not a fan of medjool dates, replace them with 2 tablespoons of raw honey, maple syrup or coconut nectar.

Avocado Dreamboat

>>>>>

I know 'avocado smoothie' sounds weird, but trust me, it will make your smoothies the best consistency ever, plus your body will soak up the avo's amazing fibre, vitamins and healthy fats.

1 avocado

1 frozen banana

2 tablespoons extra-virgin coconut oil, melted

2 large handfuls of baby spinach

½ vanilla pod, split and seeds scraped

500 ml (2 cups) coconut cream

2 tablespoons desiccated coconut

2 tablespoons coconut nectar

Topping

1 tablespoon shredded coconut

2 teaspoons coconut nectar

handful of berries (fresh or frozen)

Scoop out the avocado and place in your blender with the banana, coconut oil, spinach, vanilla seeds, coconut cream, desiccated coconut and coconut nectar. Process until silky smooth.

Pour into glasses and top with a sprinkle of shredded coconut, a drizzle of coconut nectar and a few berries of your choice. It's hard to believe such a sweet treat can be so amazingly good for you!

Serves 2

TIPS

If you don't have any coconut nectar, you can substitute the same amount of raw honey, maple syrup or 3 drops of stevia if you're a fan. It's all good. Also, if you're out of vanilla pods, use ¼ teaspoon of pure vanilla powder instead. Coconut cream is full-cream coconut milk (it is thicker and contains more coconut fats).

Happy Green Goodness

This green juice is perfect for getting you going and making you feel like you're cleaning yourself out. It packs a flavour punch and tastes super zingy!

2 handfuls of baby spinach

1 lebanese cucumber

1 granny smith apple

1 lime

handful of coriander leaves

handful of mint leaves

2 cm piece of ginger

Pop all your ingredients in the juicer and blend together.

Pour into glasses and you're good to go.

Serves 2

TIP
If you have a super strong juicer then try keeping the skin of the lime on (provided it's organic) for added bioflavonoids (anti-inflammatories that help absorb vitamin C).

Minty Matcha Magic

Matcha green tea is all the rage at the moment and I can see why – it's jam-packed with antioxidants and is a brilliant addition to your morning smoothie creations.

1 teaspoon matcha green tea

handful of mint leaves, plus extra to serve

1 frozen banana

75 g (½ cup) cashew nuts, soaked for 2 hours or overnight, then rinsed

500 ml (2 cups) almond milk

Pop everything into the blender and whiz together until smooth.

Pour into bowls or glasses and top with a few extra mint leaves. Magic!

Serves 2

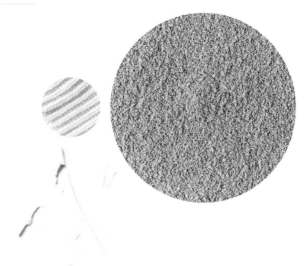

Pineapple and Mint Sunshine

This is the perfect summer creation. If you feel like making it a bit cheeky, you could easily turn it into an alcoholic slushie ...

320 g (2 cups) roughly chopped pineapple, plus extra to serve

500 ml (2 cups) coconut water

¼ bunch of mint, leaves picked, plus extra to serve

juice and zest of 1 lime

2 tablespoons maple syrup

½ cup ice cubes

Pop the pineapple, coconut water, mint, lime juice and zest, maple syrup and ice in the blender. Process until it looks like a Slurpee (you don't want this one silky smooth).

Pour into bowls or glasses and top with a little extra pineapple and a few mint leaves.

Serves 2

TIP
When you're chopping up the pineapple, be sure to use the core too. It's full of bromelain, a super healthy enzyme that aids digestion and also has a potent anti-inflammatory effect on the body.

Green Love Bowl

I love green smoothies, but for me the texture is everything — they have to be really
so I often make mine quite thick.

2 frozen bananas

100 g (1 cup) rolled oats

2 large handfuls of baby spinach

2 tablespoons extra-virgin coconut oil, melted

125 ml (½ cup) coconut water

75 g (½ cup) cashew nuts, soaked for 2 hours or overnight, then rinsed

45 g (¼ cup) medjool dates, pitted

pinch of cayenne pepper

½ teaspoon ground cinnamon

Topping

1 tablespoon shredded coconut

30 g (¼ cup) goji berries

1 tablespoon roughly chopped cashew nuts

2 tablespoons bee pollen (optional)

Pop all the smoothie ingredients in the blender and whiz everything together until you have a thick, smooth consistency and all the lumpy bits are gone.

Pour into bowls and top with the shredded coconut, goji berries, cashews and bee pollen (if using). A masterpiece!

Serves 2

TIPS
You can use any kind of date for this recipe, but medjools are juicier and sweeter – I reckon they taste like caramel. If you don't have any shredded coconut for the top, desiccated is totally fine.

Broccoli Business

This one is full of foods from the brassica family, which are loaded with health benefits … though I bet you didn't think you'd be juicing broccoli! On that note, if you have other greens around the house, add them here – dandelion greens, spinach, mustard greens, even snow peas can go into this creation!

large handful of chopped kale

60 g (1 cup) roughly chopped broccoli

3 celery stalks

1 lime

2 cm piece of ginger

1 lebanese cucumber

Pop the kale, broccoli, celery, lime and ginger into the juicer, followed by the cucumber to push everything through.

Pour into glasses and away you go.

Serves 2

Skin Elixir

What we eat and drink can really affect our skin, and keeping it in good condition is so important. Berries are sky-high in antioxidants, which means they help prevent free radical damage (one of the causes of premature ageing), while greens like cucumber and celery with their high water content also help work wonders. On that note, try upping your water intake too – you'll be amazed what a difference it makes!

handful of mixed berries
(fresh or frozen)

2 lebanese cucumbers

2 celery stalks

1 small chilli

handful of mint leaves

Put the berries, cucumbers, celery, chilli and mint through the juicer (if you're finding it hard to get the last mint leaves through, use a little more cucumber to give them a bit of a push).

Pour into glasses and enjoy.

Serves 2

TIP
For a milder juice, remove the seeds from the chilli or use less – it's your call.

Superpowered Yogini

This is why I love smoothies so much – it's so easy to sneak in so many nutrients, and superfoods make that really simple! This is one of my jam-packed go-to meals and I sometimes even make it for dinner if I'm running out of time. But my favourite time to have this nutrient bomb is when I come home after a big yoga class. Bliss.

1 avocado

150 g (1 cup) frozen mixed berries

large handful of dark leafy greens

1 tablespoon chia seeds, soaked in water for 5–10 minutes

1 teaspoon maca powder

1 tablespoon spirulina powder

4 medjool dates, pitted

1 teaspoon ground cinnamon

500 ml (2 cups) coconut milk

Topping

1 tablespoon chia seeds

handful of mixed berries (fresh or frozen)

Scoop out the avocado and pop in the blender with the berries, greens, chia seeds, powders, dates, cinnamon and coconut milk. Whiz everything together until silky smooth (this will take at least 1 minute depending on the strength of your blender, but better this than be surprised by little lumpy bits later).

Pour into glasses or bowls and top with extra chia seeds and an extra handful of berries. Delish!

Serves 2

TIPS
Use whatever dark leafy greens you have to hand here – kale, baby spinach, collard greens, silverbeet, whatever floats your boat. If you don't have coconut milk, use a nut milk like almond milk instead.

Lime and Mint Dreams

This recipe is a ripper! It keeps well in the fridge for about three days, so you could double the quantities to make enough for a few days' brekkies for yourself or to share.

1 avocado

1 granny smith apple

handful of mint leaves

4 medjool dates, pitted

juice and zest of ½ lime

500 ml (2 cups) water, plus
extra if necessary

mint sprigs, to serve

Scoop out the avocado and add to the blender with the apple, mint, dates, lime juice and water. Whiz everything together until smooth (if you find it too thick, just add a little more water).

Pour into glasses and top with the lime zest and mint sprigs. Yum!

Serves 2

TIP
I use medjool dates here, but if you want to use regular dried dates, soften them by soaking in ½ cup water or fresh apple juice first (sometimes I even throw this date juice in the combo too!).

Savoury Greens

>>>>

Sometimes when I get home and I'm completely knackered, cooking up a meal is the last thing on my mind. It's then that I turn to this. I know it might sound like a weird concept but it's kind of like having a cold soup – it makes a great quick dinner or lunch and is brilliant if you're on a cleanse, as it really fills you up and tastes surprisingly great.

1 avocado

large handful of chopped kale

large handful of baby spinach

1 lebanese cucumber

juice and zest of 1 lime

½ small chilli

2 cm piece of ginger

handful of coriander leaves

250 ml (1 cup) water, plus extra if necessary

pinch of chilli flakes, to serve (optional)

Scoop out the avocado and throw in your blender with the kale, spinach, cucumber, lime juice, chilli, ginger, coriander and water. Whiz everything together until smooth (if you find it too thick, just add a little more water).

Pour into bowls or glasses and top with the lime zest and a few chilli flakes, if you dare!

Serves 2

Alkalized Unicorn

Maybe it's just me, or maybe there's a little bit of magic involved, but I feel like when I have loads of greens like this the whites of my eyes go really clear. In any case, this super green juice will have you feeling zingy and fresh in no time.

160 g (4 cups) chopped kale

160 g (4 cups) baby spinach

2 lebanese cucumbers

large handful of mint leaves

2 granny smith apples

Put the kale, spinach, cucumbers and mint into the juicer, ending with the apples to help push everything through.

Pour into glasses and enjoy the magic!

Serves 2

Clean Green

This is a bit more hardcore than most juices as there's no apple to sweeten the deal, although the lemon, lime and ginger give it a great punch!

160 g (4 cups) baby spinach

4 celery stalks

1 lemon

1 lime

small handful of mint leaves

2 cm piece of ginger

2 lebanese cucumbers

Put the spinach, celery, lemon, lime, mint and ginger into the juicer, ending with the cucumbers to help push everything through.

Pour into glasses and you're good to go.

Serves 2

Olive Oil Green

I love extra-virgin olive oil. It contains squalene, which prevents the skin aging and is brilliant for hair health. It even helps protect the skin from UV damage!

2 frozen bananas

handful of baby spinach

4 medjool dates, pitted

pinch of ground cinnamon

handful of macadamia nuts, soaked for 2 hours or overnight, then rinsed

1 tablespoon extra-virgin olive oil

Pop everything into your blender and whiz it all together until you have a thick, smooth consistency and the olive oil is dispersed evenly (at least 1 minute depending on your blender).

Pour into bowls or glasses and away you go.

Serves 2

TIP
I like to use a mild-flavoured extra-virgin olive oil here so the taste isn't too overpowering, but feel free to experiment to see what works for you.

Oranges
& Lemons

Hangover Blaster

This one will have you feeling fresh in a flash. It's pretty full on though, so if you're the type who feels a bit nauseous after a big night out then maybe leave it till a little later in the day ...

2 lemons

2 yellow grapefruit

4 cm piece of ginger

Pop the lemons, grapefruit and ginger in the juicer, then pour into glasses. Bottoms up!

Serves 2

TIP
Try not to discard the white pith when peeling your citrus fruits here – yes, it tastes bitter but that's where loads of the health benefits are!

Pretty Passiona

This one is fresh but still creamy. And it looks super pretty too! Passionfruit seeds are high in zinc, which is kind of like one of the traffic controllers of the body – helping out our immune systems, our skin, even our brain function.

1 frozen banana

pulp of 3 passionfruit

¼ bunch of mint, leaves picked, plus extra to serve

4 medjool dates, pitted

1 tablespoon maca powder (optional)

500 ml (2 cups) almond milk

Pop the banana, passionfruit, mint, dates, maca powder (if using) and almond milk in your blender and whiz together until silky smooth.

Pour into glasses and top with a few extra mint leaves. Beautiful!

Serves 2

TIP
This recipe also works really well if you swap the almond milk for coconut water.

Golden Goodness

This one is inspired by visits to one of my favourite health spots in Bondi. The Health Emporium makes these next level smoothies and they always write sweet messages on the cups. I'm a sucker for all that cute stuff.

2 frozen bananas

2 frozen mango cheeks

½ teaspoon ground turmeric

2 cm piece of ginger

handful of macadamia nuts, soaked for 2 hours or overnight, then rinsed

4 medjool dates, pitted

500 ml (2 cups) coconut milk

Pop everything into the blender and process until super smooth.

Pour into glasses and drink up!

Serves 2

TIPS
If you don't have any fresh ginger handy, try using ½ teaspoon ground ginger instead. Almond milk makes a good substitute for coconut milk.

Digestive Broom

This one is great for getting the digestive system working properly. It's full of bromelain, a mixture of enzymes found in pineapple that aid digestion – just don't leave out the core, as that is where most of it is found. Likewise, the pectin found in the apple is a great source of fibre, but you need to keep the skin on to get the most benefits.

320 g (2 cups) roughly chopped pineapple

1 lime

2 cm piece of ginger

1 granny smith apple

Pop the pineapple, lime and ginger in the juicer, followed by the apple to help push everything through.

Pour into glasses and enjoy.

Serves 2

TIP
Using a green apple here will help stimulate the digestion, but if you only have a red apple to hand then you can always pop it in instead – its high antioxidant count will do a brilliant job too.

Piney Tropicana

Smoothies are a great way of getting loads of nutrients on board without sacrificing fibre content, plus they are so quick to prepare. (Sometimes when I practise yoga in the evenings I'm too 'yoga stoned' to cook when I get home, so I whip up a smoothie and that's my dinner done in 5 minutes). This one is super summery, and is great to make when pineapples and mangoes are in season.

1 frozen banana

230 g (1 cup) chopped pineapple

200 g (1 cup) chopped mango

large handful of baby spinach (optional)

500 ml (2 cups) coconut water

2 tablespoons extra-virgin coconut oil, melted

1 tablespoon chia seeds, to serve

Pop the banana, pineapple, mango, spinach (if using), coconut water and coconut oil in your blender and process until silky smooth.

Pour into glasses and sprinkle over the chia seeds. Ta da!

Serves 2

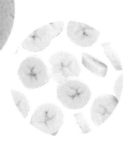

TIP
Adding baby spinach to this smoothie won't dramatically change its flavour, but it will increase the nutrients. Give it a go. You know you want to …

Pumpkin Pie

This decadent smoothie takes a little prep but it's so worth it. All you need to do is steam the pumpkin in advance – this can be done a day or two before.

400 g (1 cup) steamed pumpkin

4 medjool dates, pitted

60 g (¼ cup) almond butter

1 teaspoon pumpkin pie spice

500 ml (2 cups) almond milk

2 tablespoons maple syrup

Topping

handful of pecans

handful of pepitas (pumpkin seeds)

2 teaspoons maple syrup

Pop everything into your blender and whiz it all up until silky smooth (you can add a little extra almond milk if you feel it needs it, but I love it super thick).

Pour into glasses or bowls and top with a scattering of pecans and pepitas and a drizzle of maple syrup. Indulge!

Serves 2

TIPS
If you reduce the amount of almond milk you add to this recipe to just a few tablespoons, it will become like a thick mousse and will make an awesome dessert or sweet brekkie. If you can't find pumpkin pie spice mix, make your own by mixing together 1 tablespoon ground cinnamon, 2 teaspoons ground ginger, ½ teaspoon each ground allspice, nutmeg and clove and a pinch of ground cardamom (or mace).

Dreamy Detox

This is a great way to pack loads of goodies into one juice. It's very fresh and the parsley flavour can be quite powerful, so feel free to dial it back to suit your tastebuds. That said, parsley is one of the best sources of vitamin C and in ancient folk remedies it was used to counteract garlic breath, so it comes in handy!

4 celery stalks

1 lemon

50 g (1 cup) chopped flat-leaf parsley

2 cm piece of ginger

2 carrots

Pop the celery, lemon, parsley and ginger into the juicer, ending with the carrots to help push everything through.

Pour into glasses and you're ready to go.

Serves 2

Glorious Glower

I love this one because it's so simple and it's got a really punchy flavour. If you've got a heavy-duty juicer and you're using organic kiwifruit then leave the skin on – it'll mean extra fibre along with a whole lot of other goodies.

4 kiwifruit

1 lime

3 carrots

Pop the kiwifruit into your juicer followed by the lime and then the carrots, which will help push everything through nicely.

Pour into glasses and enjoy!

Serves 2

Ginger Twang

I love to drink this in the winter as it really warms you up, especially if you sprinkle over a little cayenne pepper at the end!

2 carrots

1 lemon

4 cm piece of ginger

2 cm piece of turmeric

2 cm piece of galangal

1 yellow grapefruit

pinch of cayenne pepper,
to serve (optional)

Pop the carrots, lemon, ginger, turmeric, galangal and grapefruit in the juicer.

Pour into glasses and sprinkle over a little cayenne pepper if you'd like a little extra punch.

Serves 2

TIPS
Galangal can be a bit tricky to find, so it's no sweat to leave it out if you can't get hold of it – it'll still taste great. Personally I don't bother peeling the ginger, galangal or turmeric, but you can if you like.

Seeing in the Dark

Yes, carrots do help you to see in the dark, and this creation will have you feeling fresh and vibrant in a jiffy. You can have this at any time of the day – I love it after an arvo yoga class and before dinner. It's pretty delicious.

2 carrots

2 oranges

1 lemon

2 cm piece of ginger

2 cm piece of turmeric

1 lebanese cucumber

Pop the carrots, oranges, lemon, ginger, turmeric and cucumber into your juicer, ending with the cucumber to help push everything through.

Pour into glasses, then sip up. Cheers, big ears!

Serves 2

The Healthy Glow

This one kind of reminds me of the veggie juices I used to get as a kid. The tomatoes help give it the perfect amount of sweetness and pop of flavour.

2 tomatoes

1 carrot

1 lemon

1 red capsicum, seeds removed

handful of basil leaves, plus extra for serving

2 celery stalks

1 lebanese cucumber

Put the tomatoes, carrot, lemon, capsicum, basil and celery into the juicer, finishing with the cucumber to help push everything through.

Pour into glasses and top with a few basil leaves. Delish!

Serves 2

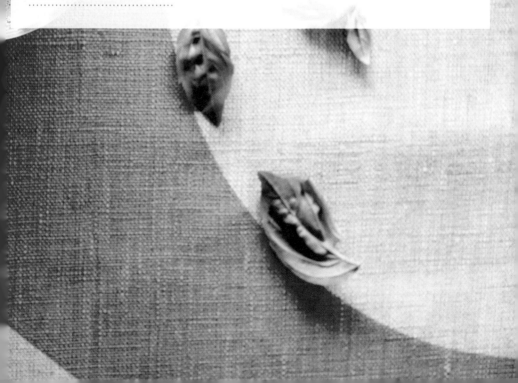

Mango–Papaya Magic

This one reminds me of living in Queensland. It's so fresh and tropical, and makes a great summer brekkie after a beach swim.

2 frozen mango cheeks

½ papaya, chopped (to give you about 1 cup)

juice and zest of 1 lime

2 cm piece of ginger (optional)

500 ml (2 cups) coconut water

½ cup ice cubes

Pop everything into the blender and process together until it looks like a Slurpee (you don't want it silky smooth).

Pour into glasses and enjoy. Pure sunshine!

Serves 2

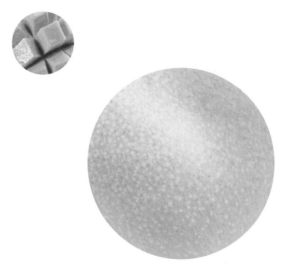

Pick-me-up

Pinks

Rosy Posy

This is just gorgeous – a little bit fancy but so worth it! Brazil nut milk is lovely in this one, too, though it can be a little tricky to find (if you have a good processor or blender try making your own).

125 g (1 cup) strawberries (fresh or frozen)

75 g (½ cup) cashew nuts, soaked for 2 hours or overnight, then rinsed

1 teaspoon rosewater

½ vanilla pod, split and seeds scraped

2 tablespoons raw honey

500 ml (2 cups) almond milk

edible rose petals, to serve

Place the strawberries, cashews, rosewater, vanilla seeds, raw honey and almond milk in your blender and process until smooth (this will smell amazing!).

Pour into glasses and top with a few rose petals. A fun, girly creation!

Serves 2

TIP
If you can't find edible rose petals, use some of the little petals you get in rose tea instead. Rosewater should be easy to find in delicatessens and health food stores. I find Indian or Middle Eastern grocers best for this.

Strawberry Kisses Cheesecake

I'm all for smoothies that taste like sweets and this one is no exception.

175 g (1 cup) strawberries (fresh or frozen)

155 g (1 cup) cashew nuts, soaked for 2 hours or overnight, then rinsed

2 tablespoons extra-virgin coconut oil, melted

2 tablespoons maple syrup

1 vanilla pod, split and seeds scraped

tiny pinch of salt flakes

500 ml (2 cups) coconut milk (or any nut milk)

Topping

handful of chopped cashew nuts

handful of chopped fresh strawberries

Pop the strawberries, cashews, coconut oil, maple syrup, vanilla seeds and salt into the blender and whiz everything together until smooth, adding the coconut milk little by little so you can have it as thick or runny as you'd like.

Pour into bowls (or glasses if you've thinned it a bit) and top with fresh cashews and strawbs. Delish!

Serves 2

Dreamy Raspberry, Lime and Coconut

This is seriously pretty, and the flavour combo is almost too good to be true! I like to make it extra thick and have it as an after-dinner treat.

270 g (2 cups) frozen raspberries

zest and juice of 1 lime

75 g (½ cup) cashew nuts, soaked for 2 hours or overnight, then rinsed

2 tablespoons extra-virgin coconut oil, melted

500 ml (2 cups) coconut milk

2 tablespoons coconut nectar

250 ml (1 cup) water (optional)

Topping

handful of fresh raspberries

1 tablespoon shredded coconut

Pop the raspberries, lime zest, lime juice, cashews, coconut oil, coconut milk and coconut nectar into your blender and process for at least 1 minute until smooth. Check the consistency and add the water little by little if you want it a bit thinner.

Pour into bowls or glasses depending on thickness and top with fresh raspberries and shredded coconut.

Serves 2

TIP
If you don't want to use cashews, macadamia nuts also work really well here.

Pomegranate Power

I love this one because it's fresh, light and it reminds me of summer. Plus the pomegranate seeds are full of antioxidants while the mint aids digestion, so it's a brilliantly healthy combo.

1 pomegranate, halved and seeds removed

175 g (1 cup) strawberries (frozen)

handful of mint leaves, plus extra to serve

1 tablespoon coconut nectar

juice and zest of 1 lime

500 ml (2 cups) coconut water

Setting a few of the pomegranate seeds aside, pop the remainder into the blender with the strawberries, mint, coconut nectar, lime juice and coconut water and whiz everything together until smooth.

Pour into glasses, top with the lime zest, the reserved pomegranate seeds and a few extra mint leaves, and away you go.

Serves 2

TIPS
You can use any sweetener you'd like here; dates, rice malt syrup, maple syrup, 3 drops of stevia or monk fruit extract – it's up to you. If it's summery and super hot try adding a few cubes of ice to this to make it even more refreshing!

Coconana–Berry Summer

This is such an awesome flavour combo. It's something I make loads of in summer, because I love to top it with fresh berries at the end.

1 frozen banana

270 g (2 cups) frozen raspberries

2 tablespoons extra-virgin coconut oil, melted

2 tablespoons desiccated coconut

2 tablespoons coconut nectar

1 vanilla pod, split and seeds scraped

250–500 ml (1–2 cups) coconut water

Topping

1 tablespoon shredded coconut

handful of fresh strawberries, chopped

handful of fresh raspberries

Pop the banana, raspberries, coconut oil, desiccated coconut, coconut nectar and vanilla seeds in the blender and process, adding the coconut water little by little until it's the thickness you like.

Pour it into bowls or glasses (depending on thickness) and top with the shredded coconut and fresh berries.

Serves 2

TIPS
I use raspberries here but you can use any berries that take your fancy, and if you can't find fresh raspberries to top your smoothie then frozen will also do the trick. If you don't have any coconut nectar, you can substitute the same amount of raw honey or maple syrup, or 3 drops of stevia, if you like.

Love Elixir

With a name and colour like this, half the fun of this one is in the making. You know what, why not say a little manifesto as you make it like, 'I created this juice with the highest love'? Hippie I know, but I think the energy we put into making our food has a huge impact on its effect on us.

350 g (2 cups) fresh strawberries

1 large beetroot

2 granny smith apples

Set aside two of the strawberries, then pop the remainder through the juicer with the beetroot and apples and pour into glasses.

Make a cut down the middle of the reserved strawberries and use to decorate the rims. Beautiful!

Serves 2

TIP
Don't freak out if, when you go to the toilet after this, things look a little redder than usual – you're not sick and it's not blood, just a natural side-effect of the beetroot.

Blood Cleanser

I love this juice because of the brilliant sweetness you get from the beetroot and the carrots. It's a real pick-me-up.

2 carrots

1 beetroot

3 celery stalks

1 lemon

2 cm piece of ginger

1 granny smith apple

Pop the carrots, beetroot, celery, lemon and ginger into your juicer followed by the apple, which will help push everything through nicely.

Pour into glasses and enjoy!

Serves 2

TIP
If your juicer's a strong one and the lemon is organic then throw the skin in too – it does make the drink a little more bitter but the health benefits are brill!

Metabolism Booster

The chilli, ginger and turmeric in this one will get your metabolism going and give your day a big old kick-start. I love making it just after yoga and before I head off into writing or meetings as I feels like it gets my head really clear and focused.

2 beetroot

1 yellow grapefruit

1 red chilli

1 cm piece of turmeric

2 cm piece of ginger

1 carrot

Put the beetroot, grapefruit, chilli, turmeric and ginger through the juicer, ending with the carrot to push everything through. Sip away!

Serves 2

TIP
To cool things down a bit, try scraping the seeds and membrane out of the chilli before juicing. You won't get quite the same warming kick, but hey, whatever works for you …

Powerhouse

Purples

Coconuts for You

My mate Jad and I created this one together when we were working at a health food store down in Melbourne. It was our morning smoothie and it tasted unreal.

150 g (1 cup) blueberries (fresh or frozen)

handful of cashew nuts, soaked for 2 hours or overnight, then rinsed

pinch of ground cinnamon

600 ml (2½ cups) coconut water

Topping

handful of fresh blueberries

Pop all the ingredients in the blender and whiz everything together until you have a silky smooth consistency.

Pour into glasses and top with extra fresh blueberries to finish. Enjoy!

Serves 2

TIP
This works really well with macadamia nuts in place of cashews if you fancy mixing things up a bit.

I Am Glowing

This creation is stuffed full of ingredients that will do your skin the world of good. Plus it tastes brill – what's not to like?

150 g (1 cup) frozen mixed berries

1 heaped tablespoon unsweetened acai berry powder

1 vanilla pod, split and seeds scraped

1 tablespoon LSA (linseed, sunflower and almond)

250 ml (1 cup) coconut milk

250 ml (1 cup) almond milk

1 teaspoon coconut sugar, coconut nectar or maple syrup

2 teaspoons sunflower seeds, to serve

Pop the berries, acai powder, vanilla seeds, LSA, coconut milk, almond milk and coconut sugar in the blender and whiz everything together until super smooth.

Pour into glasses and scatter over the sunflower seeds. Yum!

Serves 2

Blue–Narnie Wish

Blueberries probably get more publicity than any other fruit or veggie — nearly everyone knows how nutritious they are. And we all know that this flavour combo just works a treat. You really can't go wrong with a good blueberry and banana smoothie!

1 frozen banana

150 g (1 cup) frozen blueberries

2 tablespoons almond butter

1 tablespoon raw honey

625 ml (2 ½ cups) almond milk

handful of dried blueberries, to serve

Pop the banana, frozen blueberries, almond butter, honey and almond milk into the blender and whiz everything together really well until smooth.

Pour into glasses, top with the dried blueberries and get drinking.

Serves 2

TIP
If you can't get hold of dried blueberries then use whatever dried berries you have to hand – cranberries are especially great.

I'm Alive Acai

The small purple berries of the acai tree are packed full of antioxidants, which makes them brilliant for making your skin glow and helping to prevent free-radical damage in the body. An acai bowl or smoothie is a super refreshing start to the day – Hawaii is where I've tested and tried heaps of them and they just get them so spot-on there!

1 frozen banana

150 g (1 cup) frozen mixed berries

2 tablespoons unsweetened acai berry powder

500 ml (2 cups) coconut water

1 tablespoon granola, to serve

Pop the banana, berries, acai powder and half the coconut water into your blender and whiz together until silky smooth. Gradually add the rest of the coconut water until you find the thickness you love (you might not need it all).

Pour into glasses and sprinkle over a little granola to finish. Perfect!

Serves 2

TIPS
Reducing the amount of coconut water by about half will give this a really lovely thick texture. Pop it into bowls, top with a handful of fresh berries and eat with a spoon for the full 'acai bowl' experience.

Feelin' Berry Good

This recipe is probably my favourite berry recipe of all, so when blueberries aren't in season, I use frozen ones. It goes a lovely purple colour, so looks super impressive. Kids go crazy for it – my little cousins call it 'Magic Monster Goo'!

300 g (2 cups) blueberries (fresh or frozen), plus a few extra, to serve

150 g (1 cup) cashew nuts, soaked for 2 hours or overnight, then rinsed

2 tablespoons coconut nectar

2 tablespoons extra-virgin coconut oil, melted

500 ml (2 cups) coconut water

½ vanilla pod, split and seeds scraped

Pop everything into the blender and whiz until smooth (about 1 minute should do the trick).

Pour into glasses and top with a few extra blueberries. Delish!

Serves 2

TIP
If you don't have any coconut nectar you can always replace it with the same quantity of another natural sweetener like rice malt syrup or maple syrup instead.

Lucky Lavender

I know this one sounds really fancy pants, but it looks so pretty and tastes so incredible that I just had to share it with you!

300 g (2 cups) blueberries (fresh or frozen)

2 tablespoons chia seeds, soaked in water for 10 minutes

80 g (½ cup) macadamia nuts, soaked for 2 hours or overnight, then rinsed

2 tablespoons coconut nectar

2 tablespoons extra-virgin coconut oil, melted

500 ml (2 cups) coconut water

Topping

1 teaspoon chia seeds

couple of pinches of dried lavender

Place the blueberries, chia seeds, macadamias, coconut nectar, coconut oil and coconut water in your blender and process until creamy smooth.

Pour into tall glasses and top with the extra chia seeds and lavender.

Serves 2

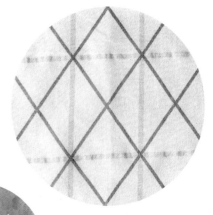

TIP
The dried lavender I use is actually organic lavender tea made from a pure, food-grade lavender. It's a wonderful calmative, and is sometimes used to treat insomnia.

Slushie

Grateful Granita

Just four ingredients make up this magical drink. I love this after a workout, or on a hot summer's day. Try it and you'll see why it hits the spot.

300 g (2 cups) frozen mixed berries

large handful of mint leaves, plus extra to serve

2 tablespoons raw honey

2 cups ice cubes

Place the berries, mint, honey and ice in the blender. Process until it looks like a Slurpee (you want it to still be nice and icy not super smooth).

Pour it into little bowls or glasses. Top each with a mint sprig and enjoy. I use a spoon when I eat this creation!

Serves 2

TIPS
Use any mix of frozen berries you like, or even just one type if you prefer. This also tastes delicious if you use coconut nectar, maple syrup, 4 pitted medjool dates, or 3 drops of stevia instead of the raw honey.

Pepper Booster

It might sound a little bizarre to use cayenne pepper in a smoothie, but don't worry – this tastes nothing like a savoury Mexican dish! The cayenne provides antioxidants, speeds up your metabolism and supports your cardiovascular system.

large handful of baby spinach

1 frozen banana

150 g (1 cup) blueberries
(fresh or frozen)

pinch of cayenne pepper

½ teaspoon ground cinnamon

3 medjool dates, pitted

75 g (½ cup) cashew nuts,
soaked for 2 hours or
overnight, then rinsed

250 ml (1 cup) almond milk

handful of fresh or frozen
berries, to serve

Pop everything except the fresh berries to serve into the blender. Process until super smooth, pour into glasses or bowls (this one's quite thick!) and top with whatever fresh berries you have to hand.

Serves 2

TIPS
If you're not a fan of medjool dates, replace them with your choice of natural sweetener, such as 2 tablespoons of maple syrup or raw honey. If you can't find any fresh berries, use dried gojis or unsweetened dried cranberries. And don't worry if you forget to soak the cashews; it won't affect the flavour, it's just to help with nutrient absorption.

Super
Naturals

Coconilla Thriller

This one is simple but it always hits the spot! I think I'm actually addicted to coconut ...

45 g (½ cup) desiccated coconut

1 tablespoon chia seeds, soaked in water for 10 minutes

60 ml (¼ cup) extra-virgin coconut oil, melted

1 vanilla pod, split and seeds scraped

4 medjool dates, pitted

500 ml (2 cups) coconut milk

Topping

1 teaspoon chia seeds

1 tablespoon shredded coconut

Pop all your goodies into the blender and give everything a good old whiz up until it's nice and silky.

Pour into glasses and top with a few chia seeds and a sprinkle of shredded coconut.

Serves 2

TIPS
If you can't get your hands on desiccated coconut, then shredded is totally fine. And remember, if you don't feel like using dates as a sweetener then you've got so many other options – maple, honey, rice malt syrup (this one's a goodie if you're staying away from fructose), stevia, monk fruit extract – the list goes on and on! Even a frozen banana will give brilliant sweetness.

Vanilla Wish

Vanilla and coconut might be considered subtle flavours on their own, yet together they are a real delight! Try this one and tell me what you think.

75 g (½ cup) cashew nuts, soaked for 2 hours or overnight, then rinsed

½ vanilla pod, split and seeds scraped

2 tablespoons coconut nectar

375 ml (1½ cups) coconut milk

500 ml (2 cups) coconut water

1 tablespoon chia seeds, to serve

Place the cashews, vanilla seeds, coconut nectar, coconut milk and coconut water in your blender and process well (this combo will be a little thinner than many of the other recipes in this book).

Pour into glasses, top with chia seeds and enjoy with a drinking straw.

Serves 2

TIP
If you don't have coconut nectar, you can always use the same quantity of raw honey, maple syrup or rice malt syrup instead. Remember, this is your creation, so use whatever works best for you.

Cookie Dough Cake Batter

Sometimes I pop my smoothies in the freezer for 20 minutes so they become a little bit like ice cream. Try it with this one – it's epic!

1 frozen banana

1 tablespoon cacao nibs

60 g (½ cup) rolled oats

500 ml (2 cups) coconut milk

40 g (¼ cup) macadamia nuts, soaked for 2 hours or overnight, then rinsed

1 vanilla pod, split and seeds scraped

60 g (½ cup) crushed paleo choc-chip cookies or other paleo cookies

Topping

handful of choc-chip cookies, crushed

sprinkle of cacao nibs

Throw the banana, cacao nibs, oats, coconut milk, macadamias, vanilla seeds and cookies in the blender and whiz everything together until smooth. Pour into glasses or bowls and top with cacao nibs and extra crushed cookies. Heaven.

Serves 2

TIP
I like to bake my own delish paleo choc-chip cookies for this recipe but you can always use good shop-bought paleo cookies — just check to make sure they're not full of preservatives or other nasties! Even just the raw cacao nibs will help give it that choc-chip feel.

Bananarama

A hands-down favourite, this is my go-to smoothie. Bananas are a brill source of the amino acid tryptophan, which converts to serotonin – a neurochemical which makes us feel happy. It's no surprise really, given that bananas kind of look like a smile!

2 frozen bananas

1 heaped tablespoon LSA (linseed, sunflower and almond)

pinch of ground cinnamon

pinch of freshly ground cardamom

3 medjool dates, pitted

500 ml (2 cups) almond milk

Pop the bananas, LSA, cinnamon, cardamom, dates and 250 ml (1 cup) of the almond milk into the blender and whiz everything together until smooth, then add the rest of the almond milk little by little until you find the perfect texture for you (you might not need all of it if you like it thick).

Pour it into bowls or glasses depending on thickness and away you go

Serves 2

Banoffee Beauty

Banoffee pie is my absolute favourite treat so I thought, why not turn it into a smoothie and enjoy it all the time?

2 frozen bananas

4 medjool dates, pitted

2 tablespoons almond butter

pinch of ground cinnamon

80 g (½ cup) macadamia nuts, soaked for 2 hours or overnight, then rinsed

250 ml (1 cup) almond milk

Topping

1 medjool date, pitted and quartered

1 teaspoon maple syrup

½ frozen banana, cut into discs

pinch of ground cinnamon (optional)

Throw the bananas into your blender with the dates, almond butter, cinnamon, macadamias and half of the almond milk. Whiz everything together, then slowly add the remaining almond milk until you get the thickness that's just right for you.

Pour into bowls or glasses (depending on thickness) and top with the chopped date, an extra drizzle of maple syrup, a few frozen banana discs and a little extra pinch of cinnamon if you like. Enjoy!

Serves 2

I Figgin' Love Oats

I love figs, dates, oats and spices, so I just had to come up with a smoothie combo that included them all. This one has awesome fibre and minerals from the dried fruit, not to mention the antioxidants from adding spices. If you're into spicy things like chai, then this will rock your socks!

2 frozen bananas

90 g (½ cup) dried figs

80 g (½ cup) pitted medjool dates

100 g (½ cup) rolled oats

30 g (¼ cup) pecans, soaked for 2 hours or overnight, then rinsed

pinch of ground nutmeg

½ teaspoon ground cinnamon

2 tablespoons maple syrup

750 ml (3 cups) almond milk

Topping

2 tablespoons pecans, chopped

2 tablespoons rolled oats

2 dried figs, roughly chopped

2 medjool dates, pitted and roughly chopped

2 teaspoons maple syrup

pinch of ground cinnamon

Throw everything except the topping ingredients into your blender and process until silky and smooth (about 60 seconds). Pour into bowls or glasses and sprinkle with the extra pecans, oats, figs and dates. Top it off with a drizzle of maple syrup and a lucky shake of cinnamon. Unbeatable!

Serves 2

TIPS
Don't worry if you don't have time to soak the pecans, it won't affect the texture or taste (it just activates the nuts so the nutrients get into your system faster). And if you prefer your smoothie in a glass, add another cup of almond milk.

Cheeky Chai Spice

By now, you've probably figured out that I have a thing for spices, and this smoothie is no exception! Spices stimulate our circulatory system, which helps to warm us up – perfect in winter.

1 frozen banana

4 medjool dates, pitted

2 tablespoons almond butter

½ teaspoon chai spice mix
(see Tip)

500 ml (2 cups) almond milk

Topping

pinch of chai spice mix

1 teaspoon chopped almonds

Pop the banana, dates, almond butter, spices and almond milk in your blender and whiz till smooth.

Pour into glasses and serve topped with an extra pinch of chai spice and a sprinkle of chopped almonds.

Serves 2

TIP

Chai is traditionally a black tea loaded with spices. I like to create my own chai spice mix by combining ¼ teaspoon each of ground cinnamon, nutmeg, ginger, cardamom and star anise. It's great here and is also lovely added to a cup of green tea.

Apple Crumble

This actually tastes like a treat! It's the best and if I'm honest I do actually make it super thick after dinner sometimes so for dessert.

250 ml (1 cup) unsweetened apple sauce

250 ml (1 cup) almond milk

80 g (½ cup) cashew nuts, soaked for 2 hours or overnight, then rinsed

1 teaspoon ground cinnamon

½ teaspoon ground allspice

¼ teaspoon ground nutmeg

4 medjool dates, pitted

Topping

handful of chopped macadamia nuts

2 teaspoons maple syrup

Put all the ingredients into your blender and whiz until smooth.

Pour into bowls or glasses and top with a scattering of chopped macadamias and a lovely drizzle of maple syrup.

Serves 2

TIPS
Stewed apples also work well here, if you have any leftover from an apple crumble proper. If you've got time, try cooking your macadamias in 2 tablespoons each of coconut oil and maple syrup in a preheated oven at 180°C for 10–15 minutes – it'll make the house smell amazing and will give you the tastiest little sprinkling topping, which also makes a brill snack on its own.

Nuts for Narnies

Bananas and macadamias are two of my favourite foods, so it's lucky I live in Australia where we grow loads of both! Macadamia nuts are high in fibre, calcium and monounsaturated fats (the good guys), and make excellent brain food.

2 frozen bananas

4 medjool dates, pitted

80 g (½ cup) macadamia nuts, soaked for 2 hours or overnight, then rinsed

2 tablespoons chia seeds, soaked in water for 10 minutes (optional)

½ teaspoon ground cinnamon

pinch of ground nutmeg

500 ml (2 cups) almond milk

Topping

½ banana, sliced diagonally into slivers

pinch of ground cinnamon

Place the bananas, dates, macadamia nuts, chia seeds (if using), spices and almond milk into the blender and process until smooth.

Pour into glasses and top with fresh banana slivers and a pinch of cinnamon. Yum!

Serves 2

TIPS

If macadamias aren't your thing, this recipe works really well with cashews too. And if you don't want to use dates, switch them for 2 tablespoons of raw honey, coconut nectar or maple syrup, or 3 drops of stevia.

Dirty Speed Date

This recipe was inspired by a trip to Adelaide when I visited this awesome health spot called Nutrition Republic and they offered me a drink called a Dirty Date, which was a date smoothie with cacao. With a name like that, how could you refuse? The extra coffee makes it a speed date – the perfect kick-start for first thing in the morning.

4 medjool dates, pitted

1 frozen banana

1 tablespoon almond butter

1 teaspoon raw cacao powder

30 ml (1 shot) espresso coffee

500 ml (2 cups) almond milk

Pop everything into your blender and whiz it all together.

Pour into glasses and off you go.

Serves 2

TIP
While I love almond butter, if you want to shake things up a bit you can always switch it for peanut butter like they do in Adelaide.

Carob Halva Heaven

This recipe makes a star of carob powder, which is one of those goodies that doesn't get used enough. It's a great source of fibre and is full of loads of minerals including magnesium, which we need for all sorts of things – from helping to relax muscles to combating stress and regulating blood sugar levels.

2 frozen bananas

2 tablespoons hulled tahini

½ teaspoon ground cinnamon

2 tablespoons carob powder

2 tablespoons raw honey

500 ml (2 cups) almond milk

Topping

2 teaspoons sesame seeds

pinch of ground cinnamon

Place the bananas, tahini, cinnamon, carob powder, raw honey and almond milk in the blender. Process until smooth, pour into glasses and top with sesame seeds and cinnamon. Hashtag yumbo!

Serves 2

TIP
When it comes to smoothies I often prefer to add hulled tahini so the flavour isn't too overpowering, but you can use unhulled if you don't mind the strong taste and want the extra fibre and nutrients.

After Dinner Mint

This combo is not only great for antioxidants and digestion, it will also give you a totally natural energy boost. Cacao is a natural source of caffeine, so it's a great pick-me-up, but it's maybe not best had last thing at night – try to keep this as a daytime drink. I love making it after a run first thing in the morning.

1 frozen banana

large handful of mint leaves

75 g (½ cup) cashew nuts, soaked for 2 hours or overnight, then rinsed

2 tablespoons cacao nibs

25 g (¼ cup) raw cacao powder

2 tablespoons maple syrup

500 ml (2 cups) almond milk

Topping

2 teaspoons cacao nibs

2 mint sprigs

Pop the banana, mint leaves, cashews, cacao nibs and powder, maple syrup and almond milk into the blender and process until everything is smooth except for the nibs (the idea is to keep a nice crunch).

Pour into glasses and top each with an extra sprinkle of cacao nibs and a sprig of fresh mint.

Serves 2

TIP
Cacao nibs are just finely chopped cacao beans. If you're struggling to hunt them down then pop some cacao beans in your coffee grinder to whip up some super fresh nibs of your very own.

Coconut Rough

Chocolate and coconut – another match made in heaven! Some people freak out when I tell them how much coconut oil I consume in a day, but I can promise you this is healthy stuff. Yes, it's a saturated fat, but it's a medium-chain saturated fat so the body uses it for energy rather than storing it. Plus your skin glows and your hair feels soft and luscious – an added bonus!

1 frozen banana

4 medjool dates, pitted

150 g (1 cup) cashew nuts, soaked for 2 hours or overnight, then rinsed

2 tablespoons desiccated coconut

35 g (¼ cup) raw cacao powder

2 tablespoons extra-virgin coconut oil, melted

500 ml (2 cups) coconut water

2 teaspoons shredded coconut, to serve

Place the banana, dates, cashews, coconut, cacao, coconut oil and coconut water in the blender and process until silky.

Pour into glasses, top with a sprinkle of shredded coconut and enjoy this coconut–chocolate masterpiece!

Serves 2

Mexicana Chocolate

I just had to create a smoothie with my two favourite things: chocolate (with its magnesium and awesome taste) and chilli (the metabolism booster and cardio-support spice). Give it a try!

2 frozen bananas

2 tablespoons almond butter

25 g (¼ cup) raw cacao powder

pinch of cayenne pepper

2 tablespoons raw honey

500 ml (2 cups) almond milk

Topping

pinch of raw cacao powder

pinch of chilli flakes (optional)

Pop the bananas, almond butter, cacao, cayenne, raw honey and almond milk into the blender. Process until lovely and smooth.

Pour into glasses and top with extra cacao powder and the tiniest pinch of chilli flakes – if you're game!

Serves 2

Monkey Magic

This smoothie tastes like dessert, it's that good. It's one of my absolute favourites and it's so, so easy.

2 frozen bananas

25 g (¼ cup) raw cacao powder

4 medjool dates, pitted

500 ml (2 cups) almond milk

Pop the bananas, cacao, dates and half the almond milk in the blender and whiz the lot together until smooth. Add the rest of the almond milk bit by bit until the texture is just right for you (if you like it thick then you won't need it all).

Pour into bowls or glasses and you're good to go!

Serves 2

TIPS
If you don't fancy dates, switch them out for 2 tablespoons of maple syrup, coconut nectar or raw honey, or 3 drops of stevia instead. And don't forget to peel those bananas before freezing them!

Thanks

- Mary Small, for surprising me with this dream project. I love every single second I get to work with you! You're one of the most inspiring and down-to-earth humans I've come across. It's such a dream come true to work together.
- Clare Marshall, for having such a calm and happy vibe on set, and for helping to create the magic of this book.
- Charlotte Ree, thank you for your passionate drive, captivating quirk and awesome fashion sense. You're so much fun to work with!
- Lauren Miller, for taking a chance and signing me. Without you these dreams wouldn't be coming true.
- Lee Lee Sutherland. Oh, Lee Lee, you're a mate I feel so lucky I have. So excited to see the next part of your journey unfold. Thank you so much for your consistent support!
- Hayley, thank you for taking me under your wing this year. You're like a positive version of Ari Gold!
- Tallulah McAloon. Lovely T, thank you for always looking out for me. P.S. Here's to loving Made in Chelsea!
- Dad, you're always there supporting the dream no matter how out there it seems. You always seem to believe in it, and that means more than you'll ever know.
- Mum, for being super positive and instilling health as a priority at such a young age.
- Linda Raymond, for believing in me no matter what and kicking me up the butt when I need it.
- Tristo! Baby bro, you're chasing dreams in your own way and that's awesome to see.
- Oscar Gordon, you not only make me laugh so much (great ab workout), but you've got such a real heart and that's rare. It's your secret weapon!
- Karina Duncan, honestly, where would I be without you? You're like my little good luck charm and you blow me away with your amazing work. I feel so lucky to be seeing your dreams come true.
- Michelle Mackintosh, you're the touch of magic that bring this book together (and you're a very good flower braider). Your genuine heart with everything you do is very inspiring.
- Hannah Marshall, best hair and make-up in town! You always make me feel pretty, especially when I don't.
- Chris Middleton, thanks for taking the snaps and helping find that magic on set.
- Tim O'Keefe, you're one talented soul. I love every chance I get to work with you. You're such a chiller who captures moments, never change that. You're one in a million.
- Simon Davis, thanks for editing this creation and making sure the smoothie names weren't too cheeky.

- Emma Christian, you work super hard and it shows. Always love it when we get to work together.
- Rivis Donnelly, every time I walk into Dymocks Collins Street your warm smile greets me and I can't thank you enough for always being so welcoming and supportive of me.
- Charlie Goldsmith. I'm always your number one spud, CG, thank you for inspiring me to live the dream.
- Leisel Jones, thank you for always bringing a smile to my day, chicken. You're such a sweet, bright soul.
- Dan Adair, you've been a huge inspiration and solid rock throughout the ups and downs. I'm so grateful. Best PT ever.
- Faustina Agolley, soul sis! Love our hangs and chats. You're such a good egg . . . a pink dolphin, some would even say!
- Lisa Mitchell. Lovely Lisa, thank you for sharing this journey. Here's to living the dream.
- Pomp and Splendour, thank you for such a pretty flower crown, made with love and passion.
- Cecilia Fox, thank you for making another stunning flower crown. I always feel like I'm a princess from a magical world when I wear one of your creations.
- Gorman, thank you for the sweet frocks. It was so hard to return them as they were all amazing!
- Husk, for the sweet outfits and stunning bling. I always feel happy wearing Husk.
- Free People, for the whimsical numbers. I felt like an ethereal forest dweller, love them!
- Bonnie and Neill, your linens bring so much character and heart to the images. Thank you so much.
- Lucy Roach, I'll be thanking you forever. You were the first person to take a chance on me; thank you so much.
- Kate Kendall, for being such a wise yogi bud. I have loved seeing your dreams come to life and to be able to share some of this journey with you means loads.
- Jad Patrick, for listening to my crazy rants and still making sense of everything. Thank you for being such a brill mate!
- Sophie Ball, when you told me to start doing the things that make me happy, that had a huge impact on me. I will always be grateful, thank you so much.
- Maddie Dixon, my whimsical nature bud. Always got to trust the heart, always.
- Avis Cheung, for always having my back and working hard to make things happen.
- Kane Dignum, for teaching me to spread my wings.

Leading Australian nutritionist Lola Berry appears regularly on television shows such as *The Project*, *The Today Show* and *A Current Affair*. She is a spokesperson on nutrition and general wellbeing in print, on radio, and to thousands of followers online.

Lola devised the simple yet groundbreaking 20/20 Diet, based on her own personal weight journey and many years' experience helping people shed excess kilos. She is the author of four bestselling books: *Inspiring Ingredients*, *The 20/20 Diet*, *The 20/20 Diet Cookbook* and *The Happy Cookbook*.

Health to Lola is a way of life. The way she sees it, every day you get to decide how you want to nourish your body, mind and soul. It's all up to you and it's easier than you think!

lolaberry.com
facebook.com/lolaberryX
instagram.com/yummololaberry
snapchat: yummololaberry
twitter.com/yummololaberry

A Plum book
First published in 2015 by
Pan Macmillan Australia Pty Limited
Level 25, 1 Market Street,
Sydney, NSW 2000, Australia

Level 1, 15–19 Claremont Street,
South Yarra, Victoria 3141, Australia

Text copyright © Lola Berry 2015
Photographs copyright © Chris Middleton 2015, except for
images on pages 30, 35, 36, 39, 41, 43, 47, 60, 62, 65, 66, 68, 71,
80, 88, 93, 94, 96, 103, 111, 116, 129, 130, 133, 134, 142 and 145
© Shutterstock

The moral right of the author has been asserted.

Design by Michelle Mackintosh
Edited by Simon Davis
Index by Lucy Malouf
Photography by Chris Middleton
Prop and food styling by Karina Duncan
Food preparation by Emma Christian
Typeset by Pauline Haas
Colour reproduction by Splitting Image Colour Studio
Printed and bound in China by 1010 Printing International Limited

A CIP catalogue record for this book is available from the
National Library of Australia.

*Please note that some of the recipes in this book have appeared
previously in* The Happy Cookbook.

The publisher would like to thank the following for their
generosity in providing props and clothing for the book:
Bonnie and Neil, Cecilia Fox, Free People, Gorman, Husk,
Indigo, Lululemon and Pomp and Splendour.

10 9 8 7 6 5 4 3 2 1